AMISH
HOUSEHOLD
TIPS

Publications International, Ltd.

A Safe Haven

When non-Amish (whom the Amish call the "English") visit Amish homes, they are struck by the tranquility that they find inside. Even in the midst of a large gathering, there is a certain quietness in the air. In an Amish household, things are never rushed, and pleasant order prevails.

This order is maintained through keeping to a rather strict schedule for all household chores. It is typical, for instance, to see freshly laundered items flapping in the breeze in an Amish yard on Mondays and Fridays. Saturdays are most often the weekly cleaning day, when rugs are shaken out, floors are mopped, and windows are washed to a sparkling shine.

The routines in different Amish households vary somewhat, and neighbors learn from each other. A favorite motto among Amish ladies is "We are never too old to learn!" As the Amish do not have health insurance, home remedies are prized and shared in an effort to keep pricey doctor's visits to a minimum.

Bring some of these remedies and hints into your own home with *Amish Household Tips.* The ideas on the following pages will help bring order to every area of your home, from the basement to the bathroom to the kitchen.

Amish families—like many other families—value being immersed in a simple, organized atmosphere at all times. They make it a point to maintain cleanliness and order in their homes. For what is a house but a sure safe haven for all who call it home?

An Inviting Kitchen

The kitchen is the busiest room in the Amish household. Most Amish homes have large kitchens with sizable tables because Amish families take turns hosting the extended family's monthly gathering, which can involve anywhere from a dozen to up to a hundred people. The Amish make a point of keeping their kitchens neat and clean so they are always ready to host these gatherings. Keeping the kitchen orderly takes organization and help from the whole family, but it is possible!

Well-Kept Cabinets

A simple cleaning solution for wood cabinets and woodwork is ¼ cup white vinegar, 1 tablespoon shampoo, and 1 gallon warm water. Using a soft cloth, wipe cabinets down with this mixture.

Amish kitchens are subject to significant mess and clutter from cooking, baking, and canning.

Are some areas of you cabinets difficult to access and clean? Use an old toothbrush to brush dirt out.

Shiny Countertops

For polished countertops that gleam, use a mixture of 2 tablespoons ammonia, 3 tablespoons liquid dish detergent,

1 pint rubbing alcohol, and enough water to make a gallon. Keep some handy in a spray bottle for quick cleanup.

❧ If permanent marker has made its way onto your kitchen counters, don't despair. Apply a little rubbing alcohol to a paper towel, and rub area until the mark is gone.

A Spotless Oven

❧ For easy cleanup after an oven spill, pour a small amount of water on the spill while the oven is still warm. Wait 30 minutes, then wipe up the spill with ease.

❧ Grease and oil from cooking can build up into a thick film on the glass of the oven door. To remove this film, rub the inside of the window with a sponge soaked in distilled white vinegar. Let vinegar sit for 20 minutes, then wipe glass again with a cloth soaked in warm, soapy water. Stand back and admire your sparkling glass!

❧ If your oven racks are sticking, use steel wool pads to rub the ridges along the oven walls. Wipe ridges down with a wet cloth, and allow the areas to dry. Wipe down again with a cloth dipped in vegetable oil, and the racks will glide smoothly.

> Because the Amish always eat together as a family, many hours are spent around the kitchen table.

❧ To clean burned-on foods from broiler pans, just heat the pan and sprinkle laundry detergent on it. Cover pan with paper towels soaked in hot water, and let sit 1 hour. Remove towels and wipe gunk off easily.

A Shiny Sink

❀ Combine lemon and baking soda for the ultimate cleaner! Sprinkle baking soda on the fleshy side of a lemon half, rub down the entire sink with it, then rinse.

❀ To shine your stainless steel sink and appliances, use a mixture of 2 tablespoons ammonia, 3 tablespoons liquid dish detergent, 1 pint rubbing alcohol, and enough water to make a gallon. Pour mixture into a bottle and spray on surfaces. Wipe areas down with a dry cloth.

❀ Another way to shine stainless steel appliances is to rub a small amount of olive oil over the surfaces with a soft cloth, then go back over the areas with another cloth dampened with vinegar.

Refresh the Fridge

❀ Clean fridge interior with a mixture of ¼ cup vinegar and 1 gallon warm water. The vinegar will clear out any old food odors, and its scent will evaporate quickly.

❀ Don't forget to keep the refrigerator handle clean—it's a germ magnet. Use disinfectant wipes on it every other day to keep bacteria from lingering.

> Never use soap to clean the inside of your refrigerator. Soap leaves a scent behind that your food might absorb.

🌼 To remove fridge odors, crumble a few pieces of newspaper and place them in the back of the fridge. Any odor should be gone within 3 days.

Tame Stains

🌼 If your hard water has left you with stained glassware, soak the stained items overnight in a solution of a handful of salt and a quart of white vinegar. All you'll have to do in the morning is wipe them clean!

🌼 Remove tea stains fast! To eliminate them, cut a lemon into quarters and dip 1 piece into salt. Squeeze some juice into the teapot and rub interior with the lemon piece. The lemon breaks up the tannin, and the salt acts as an abrasive to make the stains disappear. When you are satisfied that the stain is gone, wash the teapot in hot, soapy water.

🌼 Having trouble getting a price sticker off a piece of glassware? Gently rub the sticker with a cloth dipped in olive oil until the sticker becomes saturated, then use a razor blade to remove the sticker completely.

🌼 If a knife or any other kitchen utensil becomes rusty, grab an onion and start chopping. The acid in the onion will break down the rust, leaving you with a rust-free tool!

MEMY Spill something on your cookbook? Blot the pages dry with paper towels, then slip pieces of waxed paper between any affected pages before closing the cookbook. The waxed paper will keep the pages from sticking together until they dry completely.

Cracks and Scratches

MEMY To get rid of a scratch on a drinking glass or glass vase, rub the scratch with non-gel white toothpaste and a soft cloth. The paste's abrasive properties will smooth the scratch away.

MEMY To seal cracks in china and ceramics, place the damaged piece in a pan of milk and boil for 45 minutes. The milk forms a tight seal and heals the crack, making your dish as good as new!

A Homey Feel

Many Amish women enjoy creating an inviting kitchen through precise placement of nice bowls and baskets with pretty doilies underneath. Having only a few such things on the counters creates a comfy—but uncluttered—room. Use the baskets to store utensils, napkins, spices, or potpourri.

All Things
Come Clean Again!

The Amish typically have a couple of "laundry days" each week (often Mondays and Fridays, with one of the days devoted to laundering clothes and the other day devoted to washing sheets and other household items). Laundry tasks are usually divided among the women in the family, thus lightening the load. Some grumbles about helping out can usually be heard from the children along the way, but it is hoped that they, too, will someday appreciate what a blessing it is to have a healthy family that dirties lots of clothes!

Washing Tips

❧ Prevent colors from bleeding by adding 2 tablespoons salt to the washing machine with your detergent.

❧ To get white cotton and linens back to their crisp, bright look, mix ¼ cup salt and ¼ cup baking soda with 1 gallon water in a large pot. Bring to a boil, then turn off the heat. Add the yellowed items and let them sit for 1 hour. Rinse items, then hang them out to dry.

> While doing laundry, the Amish often reflect upon their thankfulness for living in a place where water is abundant.

Wringer Washers

Many Amish still use wringer washers to do their laundry. These washers are powered with generators or gasoline engines. For the wringer washers to empty properly, the machines need to be located in a cemented room with a drain. Many Amish laundry rooms are attached to the kitchen. If an Amish home does not have an attached laundry room, laundry is usually done in the basement.

A good alternative for fabric softener is to add 1 cup white vinegar to rinse water.

Stains Be Gone!

Sweat

For perspiration stains, make a paste of baking soda and water. Rub paste on stains before washing garment.

Rid a shirt of ring around the collar: Squirt a small amount of shampoo on stain, rub shampoo into garment, then wash item as usual.

Grass

Dab grass stains with non-gel toothpaste, rinse, and wash as usual.

Meat tenderizer also works on grass stains. Sprinkle it on the stain before washing garment.

Rust

 To rid clothes of rust stains, squeeze a glob of toothpaste over stain, rub with a damp cloth until stain is gone, then rinse item thoroughly.

Product Alternatives

• **Laundry detergent:** 1 bar Fels-Naptha, grated fine; 1 cup washing soda; 1 cup Borax. Mix ingredients together, then store in an airtight container. Use 2 tablespoons per load of laundry.

• **Fabric softener:** 2 cups white vinegar, 2 cups baking soda, 4 cups water. Mix ingredients in a 2-gallon pail (it will fizz!) using a whisk. Store in an old fabric softener container, and shake well before using ¼–½ cup per load of laundry.

• **Stain spray:** ½ cup rubbing alcohol, ½ cup hydrogen peroxide, ¼ cup clear dish-washing liquid, ¼ cup water. Add all ingredients to a spray bottle, and shake well before each use.

• **Universal stain remover:** Make a paste of equal parts baking soda and water. Paint the paste on the stain, then scrub the stained area with an old toothbrush before washing the item as usual.

Lemon juice is another proven rust remover. Moisten stain with lemon juice, cover it with salt, and let item dry in the sun before washing it as usual.

Ink and Crayon

Use rubbing alcohol to remove ink marks from clothing. Set the affected area on top of four folded paper towels. Dampen a soft white cloth with rubbing alcohol, then blot stained area to push the ink onto the paper towels.

Get crayon off clothing with WD-40. Place the garment on paper towels and spray both sides of the stain with WD-40. Next, rub liquid dish-washing soap into the stain until the crayon disappears. Launder as usual.

Hang Everything Out to Dry

Using bike rims with spring-loaded clothespins hanging from the spoke holes as hangers for underwear, socks, washcloths, and other small pieces is a handy way to dry these small items.

Hanging heavy towels on the wash line horizontally will help them dry faster. This is especially helpful in the wintertime, or on days without much breeze.

The Amish depend on fresh outdoor breezes to dry their clothes. On a warm, windy day, items hung on the line can dry in an hour or two.

Serene Spaces

As in most homes, the living spaces in Amish households always seem in need of sweeping and other upkeep. Being clean and orderly is very important to the Amish, as they view their homes as safe havens from school, farm, and workplaces. Few Amish women have jobs outside the home. They take pride in their duties as keepers of their homes, and thus they aim to present a tidy, inviting home at all times.

The Living Room
Upholstery Upkeep

꧁꧂ To clean upholstered furniture, brush it with warm, soapy water. Next, lay an old towel on the furniture. Place your palms on the towel, and press down with all of your weight. Repeat this procedure all along the towel, and keep using additional towels until furniture is clean.

The Amish do not use clothes dryers—and thus do not generally need dryer sheets— but some Amish find them handy for other household uses.

꧁꧂ To freshen upholstered furniture, place dryer sheets under the cushions. The sheets will release a pleasant smell.

Wood Renewed

꽃 Potted plants can leave water marks on your wood furniture. To prevent these stains, make a pot coaster from the plastic lid of a coffee can. Cut the edges off so it fits just under the saucer of the plant. The lid will provide an extra layer of protection while being virtually invisible to guests.

꽃 To restore wood furniture, place a tea bag in ½ cup boiling water. Steep until tea is cool. Dip a cloth into the tea, and wring out excess. Wipe furniture in the direction of the wood grain, then buff dry with a clean, soft cloth.

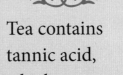

Tea contains tannic acid, which removes grime and restores shine.

An Orderly Bedroom

꽃 If your sheets have a tendency to slip, sew or use safety pins to fasten elastic bands 12–20 inches from each corner. Slip corners underneath mattress to keep sheets secure.

꽃 Short on closet space? Increase your vertical storage by installing an over-the-door towel rack on your closet door. You now have easy-access pant storage (and extra room inside your closet where your pants used to be!).

Flawless Floors
Swept Away

꽃 For dustless sweeping, put a couple of drops of baby oil on your broom before each sweeping session.

The bristles of a broom can become splayed from use. Wrap a rubber band around the broom a few inches from the bottom. Let broom sit this way for a couple of days, and it will be back in tip-top shape!

Renewal

Like most people, the Amish like to rearrange their furniture from time to time for a fresh look. To protect your floors and make heavy furniture easier to move, glue small pieces of rug on the bottoms of the legs of the furniture.

Caring for Your Carpet

If food gets spilled on your carpet, pick up any big pieces, soak up excess liquid with a paper towel, then clean the area with a baby wipe. Wipe area with a damp cloth, and let it dry.

If your carpet has an odor, sprinkle baking soda over it, let it sit for 20 minutes, then vacuum. The baking soda sinks into the fibers and helps remove deep dirt and odors.

More Flooring Tips

Use ¼ cup vinegar in a pail of warm water to mop your floors. It will make them shine.

Don't throw away that old flannel-back tablecloth. Spread it on the kitchen floor to protect it when canning tomatoes or grapes.

Useful Spaces

The Amish get a lot of use out of their basements, porches, and garages. Most Amish homes have full basements, which come in handy for hosting gatherings and church services. Because up to 200 people attend an average Amish church service, you need a space large enough to comfortably sit people to worship and to accommodate tables for the fellowship meal. Some Amish families use their garage to host these services.

Flooring Tips

Save coffee grounds to use as a sweeping compound on your cement basement or garage floors. Once they have dried out, coffee grounds work great for dust control and leave behind a pleasant smell.

Next time you get icy patches on your porches or walkways, skip the salt and sprinkle on baking soda instead. Baking soda won't harm your shoes or damage floors if tracked inside.

Do you struggle with grease spots on your garage floor? Put a thick layer of powdered laundry

Amish basements usually have canning rooms, where canned food and potatoes are stored. These rooms are kept dark and cool to help preserve these food items.

detergent on the spot, and leave it overnight. Sweep up the powder in the morning, and you'll find that the powder has absorbed all the grease.

🌾 Try using baking soda on greasy spots too. Sprinkle soda on the spot, let it sit for 20 minutes, then scrub with a wet, hard-bristled brush.

Tool Kit Care

🌾 Here's a quick fix for dull scissors: make a few cuts with the problematic pair through a sheet of fine sandpaper. The gritty surface restores the edges of the blades, making your snips as crisp as a brand-new pair.

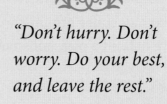

"Don't hurry. Don't worry. Do your best, and leave the rest."
—**Amish Saying**

🌾 Keep your paintbrushes supple! After using your paintbrush, rinse it in a bucket of warm water with a few drops of liquid fabric softener mixed in, then wipe bristles dry. Your paintbrush is sure to be soft and pliable for your next job.

🌾 If you have a small amount of paint left over after completing a job, preserve it for future touch-ups. Pour paint into glass baby food jars, and close lids tightly.

🌾 If you are working on a project that involves repapering a room, distilled white vinegar removes old wallpaper quickly. Dip a sponge into hot vinegar, then rub sponge all over old wallpaper. Let the vinegar work for 15 minutes, then peel wallpaper right off.

Bug Control

After cleaning your basement, put mothballs here and there to repel insects and rodents. They detest the smell.

If your basement is unfinished (as all Amish basements are), spray natural bug repellent around the perimeter of the basement once a month.

To help repel insects from your porch, wash it down with a strong-smelling pine product every week. Flies dislike the smell of pine.

Preparing for Guests

In the weeks before an Amish family hosts a gathering or church service, they give their whole dwelling a thorough cleaning from top to bottom. Though this may seem like an immense chore, they see it as a huge blessing. These semi-annual cleanings help keep their household organized and clean, and they remind them of how truly blessed they are to have a wonderful gathering space— and so many loved ones!

A Tranquil Bathroom

Contrary to popular belief, the majority of Amish do have bathrooms. In most areas, the Amish acquired indoor plumbing at approximately the same time as their English neighbors. Most Amish bathrooms have beautiful cabinetry to hold linens and toiletries. The one thing Amish bathrooms lack is electrical outlets! Many Amish use battery-powered lights or a wall-mounted gas light. An added bonus from the gas lights is that they help heat the bathroom in the wintertime and give a warm, cozy atmosphere in which to bathe.

Tips for Your Toilet

To remove water marks from your toilet bowl, pour 2 cups white vinegar into bowl and soak overnight. Give it a quick scrub with the toilet brush in the morning, flush, and your bowl will sparkle.

Also use white vinegar to clean the outside of the toilet bowl and the floor around the toilet. This eliminates odors and kills any lurking germs.

As with any large family, having only one bathroom can be difficult at times. Add a teenager or two to the mix, and timers become necessary to keep things running smoothly.

Tackle the Tub

✼ To remove soap scum, mix equal parts baking soda and water to create a paste, then brush paste on problematic areas. Let paste sit for 15 minutes. Wipe paste away with a cloth dipped in warm, soapy water to reveal a lovely, shiny tub!

✼ To minimize soap scum, consider changing soaps. Moisturizing soaps and liquid shower gels are known to leave less scum behind than most bar soaps do.

✼ To remove mold from a fabric shower curtain, brush lemon juice on affected areas, sprinkle salt on top, then rub mixture into fabric using a soft cloth. Let item sit for 3 hours, then launder as usual. The acid in the juice breaks up the mold, and the salt helps to scrub it away.

✼ To remove old tub appliqués, warm ½ cup white vinegar, then soak a cloth in the liquid. Spread dripping cloth over appliqué, and let it sit for 15 minutes. The vinegar

Homemade Shower Spray

Shower sprays help minimize soap scum. Make your own shower spray by filling a spray bottle a third of the way with white vinegar, then filling the rest of the bottle with water. Keep this spray bottle in your bathroom, and use it to liberally spray the shower after each use.

will penetrate and loosen the glue, and the appliqué will peel right off.

Difficult Drains

༄༅ Do you have a problem with clogged drains? Pour 1 cup salt, 1 cup baking soda, and 1 cup white vinegar down the drain. Let mixture foam for 10–15 minutes, then flush drain with 2 quarts boiling water.

It's All in the Details

Pedestal sinks look elegant but provide little space for keeping essentials such as toothbrushes handy. This problem can be solved using a washcloth that matches your bathroom color scheme. Fold up one side 3½ inches, sew along the sides to secure, then sew straight lines to form as many pockets as you have toothbrushes. Next, fold the top of the washcloth down 1 inch, and sew it down to create a pocket for slipping a hanger through. Hang toothbrush holder on your bathroom wall. For another nice touch, hang a small oblong wicker basket with one loop handle on the wall beneath the toothbrush holder, and use the basket to hold your toothpaste. These pieces will look nice and be functional at the same time.

꾸♠꾸 Another clog fix is to crumble two antacid tablets into drain, followed by a cup of white vinegar. Let the mixture fizz for 20 minutes, then flush drain with boiling water.

Superb Surfaces

꾸♠꾸 Use hydrogen peroxide to clean bathroom grout. Spray on, let it do its work for 10 minutes, then wipe entire area clean.

꾸♠꾸 Pour 1 cup rubbing alcohol, 1 cup water, and 1 tablespoon white vinegar into a spray bottle. Shake before using on windows and mirrors for a streak-free shine!

Squash Squeaks

꾸♠꾸 Quiet a noisy bathroom door! Put a little petroleum jelly on your hands, then rub it all over the hinges. Move door back and forth to work the jelly into the hinges. Soon, no more squeak!

꾸♠꾸 Another option for a squeaky bathroom door is to squeeze a small amount of hair conditioner onto a rag and apply it to the hinges. The conditioner will lubricate the metal, stopping the squeak. Olive oil can also be used for the same results.

Home Remedies

Home remedies are second nature to Amish homemakers. Acting as nurse to family members suffering minor maladies is certainly part of their duties. Also, as dedicated gardeners, the Amish have many natural cures at their fingertips at all times.

Conquer Colds
Liquid Remedies

✿ For relief from a head cold, drink 1 cup hot water flavored with 1 teaspoon crushed ginger and 1 teaspoon sugar.

✿ Use hot lemon tea for sweet relief from colds and coughs. Fill a cup with hot water, then add the juice from half a lemon. Sweeten this tea with honey, if desired.

A simple yet effective remedy for a sore throat is to gargle a mixture of 1 tablespoon vinegar, 1 tablespoon water, and ⅛ teaspoon salt.

Poultices

✿ To break up chest congestion, heat ¾ cup sliced onion in lard, using just enough lard to moisten onion. Simmer until onions are heated through but not browned. Put onions on a flannel cloth and place this poultice on the patient's chest.

✻ Another onion cure: Place a slice of onion on the bottom of your feet, then put a sock on over it to keep it in place. This remedy fights colds and fever.

Soothing Baths

✻ If you have a cold, add several teaspoons of ground ginger to your bathwater. Ginger works to loosen mucus and soothe inflammation.

✻ Another remedy for a head cold is a footbath, which is believed to improve circulation. Fill a basin with water as hot as you can tolerate, then add 1 tablespoon ginger and ¼ cup apple cider vinegar. Sit back, and soak away!

Relieving Headaches

✻ If you are suffering from a headache, mix the juice of one lemon into a cup of warm water. Drink every hour until you have relief.

✻ Taking a footbath in hot water to which 2 teaspoons of powdered mustard have been added can relieve headaches.

Easing Earaches

✻ An old remedy for an earache is to put several drops of peppermint oil on a cotton ball and place it in the affected ear before you go to bed. When you wake up, the pain should be gone.

Garlic is a natural antibiotic. Cut raw cloves up into small pieces and add to food and drinks to naturally purify your body. Aim for ingesting 2 cloves a day.

꧁꧂ Garlic oil is another good earache remedy. Tilt your head to the side, then put several drops of garlic oil in affected ear. After letting it set for a few minutes, put a paper towel over affected ear and tilt head to the other side to let oil drain out for a few minutes. Gently blot any excess oil. Repeat a few times a day until your ear feels better.

Feisty Fevers
Baths

꧁꧂ If your child has a fever, add 1 cup of apple cider vinegar to his or her bath.

꧁꧂ Dry mustard is also a known fever fighter. Add a spoonful of dry mustard to patient's bath for fever relief.

More Fever Remedies

꧁꧂ For quick relief from a fever, rub drops of vinegar on your forehead, temples, palms of your hands, and the bottoms of your feet. Repeat as needed every half hour.

꧁꧂ To break a fever or check a cold in its early stages, make a tonic with a cup of warm water, 2 tablespoons lemon juice, and 2 tablespoons honey.

If you are struggling with constipation, drink this natural laxative once a day: 1 pint hot water, 2 tablespoons Epsom salts, and ½ tablespoon cream of tartar.

Daunting Diarrhea

✤ For mild diarrhea, drink 1 cup blackberry or blueberry juice twice a day. *Sip blueberry juice slowly, as it has a laxative effect on some people.*

✤ Squeeze juice out of 2 lemons and add to a quart of warm water. Drink 1 cup every few hours until you feel better. This remedy usually cleanses the body of diarrhea pretty quickly.

Homemade Electrolyte Solution

When a family member is struggling with diarrhea, it is good to have an electrolyte solution on hand to prevent dehydration. Use the recipe below to mix one up in your own home.

1 quart water
3 tablespoons sugar or honey
½ teaspoon baking soda
½ teaspoon salt
lemon, lime, or fruit juice (optional)

Mix all above ingredients well. Add lemon or lime slices or a bit of fruit juice, if you like. Store in the refrigerator. Sip throughout the day until you feel better. Use each batch within a few days.

A Hodgepodge of Remedies

 Feeling run down? Add 1 tablespoon blackstrap molasses to a cup of hot water and drink. Repeat every day until you feel more energetic.

 Hiccups driving you crazy? Eat a tablespoon of peanut butter! This remedy is known to work very well.

 One easy proven remedy for head lice is mayonnaise. Use a generous amount to completely cover your hair and scalp, then wrap hair with plastic wrap. Let the mayonnaise work for an hour, then shampoo as usual. Use this treatment every other day for a week, and you should be lice free!

When struggling with lice, it is always a good idea to give all bedding, clothes, and any soft-cloth dolls a thorough washing.

Be-Healthy Tonic Recipe

Put one cup boiling water in a quart jar or a pot with a lid. Add 1½ teaspoons salt, 2 teaspoons red pepper, and 2 tablespoons honey. Cover the container and let it sit until cool. Shake or stir mixture, then add 1 cup apple cider vinegar. As a preventative, take 1 teaspoon 2 or 3 times a day. As a cure for colds, take 1 teaspoon every hour. Always stir or shake well before using.

Grooming

The Amish do not spend a lot of time on their looks, as, in their minds, an emphasis on outward appearance seeks attention and leads to excessive pride. Nonetheless, as in housekeeping and other aspects of daily living, the Amish strive to present a simple and orderly personal appearance.

Hair Care

Using vinegar to rinse your hair is a natural way to keep it in good condition.

If you struggle with dandruff, grind two aspirin and mix the crushed pills into a squirt of regular shampoo.

Before you toss an almost-empty conditioner bottle, use the last drops to make a leave-in conditioner. Fill the bottle with water, then shake and pour contents into a spray bottle.

Mind Your Mouth

It is easy to make homemade mouthwash. Simply add 1 teaspoon salt and 1 teaspoon baking soda to ½ cup water, then rinse and gargle as needed. A drop of peppermint extract can be added for a minty taste.

Soothe chapped lips by rubbing olive oil directly on your lips. Or, you can make your own lip balm: Mix 1 part olive oil and 1 part melted beeswax, then pour into an old gloss pot. Let balm harden in the fridge before using.

More Grooming Tips

 Add a teaspoon of baking soda to dishwater to keep your hands as soft as can be.

 Are you bothered by acne? Try applying tea tree oil or witch hazel to problem areas before going to bed each night.

 Do your glasses fog up in bad weather? Put a dab of shaving cream on each lens, then rub it in gently with a soft cloth. There will be no streaks left behind, and your glasses will not fog up anymore.

Worn Hands, Happy Family

Some Amish women joke about their "manicured" hands, as Amish hands are anything but manicured. Working in the garden, yard, and dairy barn can wreak havoc on hands. Nails become broken from working to keep the weeds under control in the garden. Canning season tends to be the worst time for hands: They become scratched from picking berries and purple from canning grapes. For the most part, Amish women do not worry about the looks of their hands. They see worn hands as proof that they are always hard at work caring for their families.